The Power of the Tongue

Speaking better words which create better chances.

Author/Believer: La Kadron Ivery

Table of Contents

Acknowledgments

Dear God,

It is you I desire most. It is you I thank for the times we spend together, the people you allow me to meet, the life that is given to me from you. No matter how challenging it gets, I am still driven to know more about you. I desire to fulfill the will you set for me from the day I was placed in my mother's womb. You have blessed me so much. I lean not on my own understanding. Instead I trust the unseen. I believe this is why I am here. I am here once again, approaching the 2016 Olympic Trials (when I wrote the first draft of this book).

Now I am up again facing the 2020 Olympics Trials which is now postponed to the 2021 Olympics Trials. You have blessed me to make the 2004 Olympic Trials, the 2008 Olympic Trials, the 2012 Olympic Trials, and you kept me safe as I drove thirty-one hours with my two children from Texas to Oregon with the attempt to perform at the 2016 Olympic Trials. I know you are probably wondering why I am still pushing for the record, pushing for that dream to come true. Well, I'll tell you why. Because I am your child, and what I understand is nothing is impossible with you… so here I go again… same God, same goal, different approach…

The Power of the Tongue

I, La Kadron Ivery, commit my works to you so you can make it a success according to Proverbs 16:3.

For you, Jaythen Ivery and Jaylee-Amil Ivery, and now Ivery Basileia and my husband MaShakeem Shabazz, mommy loves you, and your wife loves you, and I pray to make you proud!

To my entire village, (you know who you are), thank you so much for making this possible and being Harvest hands: Sammy Ivery, Melva Ivery, Damond Taylor, thank you for naming me "La Kadron" when you were only eight years old and Welcome Home! Audrea Taylor, Joel and Sandy Delaney, Michelle Rosenberg, Rosemary Dupree, Michael Ford, Stacy Bowers-Smith, Clyde Hart, Todd Harbor, Danny Brabham, Tim chiropractor/assistant, Dr. Shamonica Trunell-Morgan (Chiropractor), Tenika Powell, Barbara Collins, Kevin Robinson, Nadaya, Dr. Peregrine, Sckyular Cox, Deon Williams, Pastor Dr. Foreman, just a name of few.

I started this book in 2014 and completed it in 2019. Within this journey, God has brought Jaythen, Jaylee, and two new angels into our family — MaShakeem Shabazz and Ivery Shabazz. Thank you so much for joining us.

All of my work is God Given and love thy neighbor effort. The people are the focus; the children and are the hope I see and believe in.

I am grateful for the community of people who have helped me this far in my life, from family to friends to strangers passing by.

With all the love and support I have received from the union of people who support me, please know you give me inspiration to continue on the path of growth! I love you.

Reason for Writing
Power of the Tongue

Power of the Tongue came about from a previous relationship with my former spouse of 14 years. As a Baylor Graduate, a Tyler Texas Native, all my life, I have had dreams, and I have set out to pursue them with one thought in mind: "*If God is for you, who can be against you.*" At times, I even doubted whether God was for me especially in the past relationship.

Verbal abuse was common in my past relationship, yet instead of leaving, I was the type to wish for the better, pray for the better, and continue to work on my half to grow, so I would leave no excuse on the table as to why that past relationship would not work for me.

Instead of believing the negative and critical thoughts my former spouse had about me, I would take the word of God and replace it in my heart of how HE felt about me. I would take the word of God and focus on his promises. Those promises led me to this book and led me to be able to tell you that no matter what others think of you, no matter how they feel about you, there is a promise you can rely on:

"*If God is For You, Nobody Can be Against You.*"

Introduction

Welcome to The Power of the Tongue. I am so excited you are taking the time to prepare for speaking the best for you and others in your life. This is a big decision and new verbal transition in your life!

Your verbiage will be the foundation for your future in more ways than you can imagine speaking. That's why I have put together a short and straight to-the-point book to help you enhance the lines of dialogue and expand your way of speaking over your life to turn your life tests into testimonies.

It is my desire that your life will be the most rewarding, productive, satisfying, and encouraging life you are able to live. When taking God's word and his promises into your daily life, there's no telling how God will use you for his purpose and his glory.

I commit this book, "The Power of the Tongue," my works to the Lord, so He will make it a success.

Proverbs 16:3 (NIV)

Verbally Said

Since the beginning of time, it has been known the world was spoken into existence with the mighty, pink sword we all carry. I call it the concealed masterpiece. We do not need to have it registered, a license to carry it, or even pay taxes on it, yet it can start a war, cool a fire, light a heart, and carry our lives to better or worse.

What am I speaking about here? The tongue—that small, ever so threatening weapon—so ambiguous, it can carry bitterness and anger. But if used in the proper manner, it can offer to all love, peace, joy, wealth, health, desire, and the list goes on.

I am simply saying you can build and create the life, the faith, and the foundation that is stable and sound, with this one tool—the tongue.

Now stick yours out, and let's begin to explore the life you deserve, a life you have always dreamt of, a life that is promised to you by the one King who owns the nation and the land, the creator, the beginning and the end, the one who knows all, the healer, the deliverer, the most powerful of all... God. I like to refer to the three kings, as my Father, his Son, and the Holy Spirit.

Wait, wait, wait, before I lose you—stick with me here. I am not here to get you to change your religion or label yourself as a Christian or a Jew, etc. I am here to walk you through a journey of pages of greatness and truth—promises that were made for Believers. Yes, BELIEVERS, because what you may fail to know is God is in us all.

See, I was told as a young child by my father the reason we do not reach our destiny is because we search everywhere, but we forget to search inside of ourselves for the answer. The answer is in you. God is inside of you. You were created in his image. You are a GOD, you are a GODDESS. You are royalty, you are health, you are strength, you are greatness, you are peace, you are joy, you are happiness.

If you were to know more about the **I AM**, than you would invest more into becoming the **YOU ARE** you were meant to be.

Begin with speaking what you want to become, believing you were created for the better from the best. Begin with knowing the word and the world structure of success is more than just fortune, fame, and prosperity. Begin by knowing your Father measures success by the source of obedience, faith, and righteousness. You are a success! If you feel you are not, know you can be.

In the book of Isaiah 59:19, it is stated, *"When the enemy shall come in like a flood, the Spirit of the Lord shall lift up a standard against him."*

What is the standard the scripture is speaking of? The fact is what we speak is what we know, so knowing the Living Word, some call it the Good News, can be a very powerful tool while we are here on earth.

It is important to know The Word. Know the truth, know his power which enables your power as a yielding vessel to hold onto, and speak the word of truth. Do this by receiving and giving the word. You will come to realize the word is like a devouring fire as it goes forth against the enemy and destroys the powers of evil as you speak HIS WORD in faith.

As a believer, a seeker, a doer, and now a speaker, you should be able to scatter much of the darkness and battles of life as you speak truth over yourself and others. You are so powerful!

Once you realize and release your power, you will notice you are unlimited. You have the greatest genes because the genes that are in you are the genes of the Great Spirit who created the Universe in which we live, and those genes are at the core of your being.

You must take the time to come to truth, admit and submit to yourself, and be willing to admit that all things are possible. You are prepared to handle them all.

Verbal Purpose

In this book, I will expand on ways you, the reader, is capable of becoming a better version of yourself and back the facts or prophesy with scripture from the Bible. For example, it is made clear in the Bible...

"I know the plans that I have for you declares the Lord; Plans to prosper you and not to harm you, plans to give you hope and a future." (Jeremiah 29:11 NIV)

Everything in this life is predestined. The Lord Plans to Prosper you. Better yet, you are here with me, and I am here with you. You and I have another chance at this moment to get this right.

I want to see you live your best life while you are here—not waiting until you are lying in a casket hoping for the pearly white gates. This world we are allowed to live in is beautiful—full of opportunity.

You can relax, read this book, and use it as a guide with peace and pleasure, because you will be transformed into speaking with greatness. I am not asking for tithes and offering. All I am asking for is your time and commitment to knowing your power, displaying your worth, and acknowledging your greatness by simply speaking.

As I was growing up, I regularly heard the expression, *"Sticks and Stones may break my bones, but words will never hurt me."* As a young child, my mother and father would tell me you should not say things you do not mean. They would always tell me words have power when you use certain emotions behind them, and power can exercise a form of control when allowed.

As I grew older, I came to understand the meaning of the statement and the meaning behind the statement: words formed against us are only as powerful as we allow them to be. The absolute truth is our words do have power. We are able to see power manifest with the simple words we speak.

I pray the reader's tongue will bring forth healing... and he/she will guard his/her mouth according to Proverbs 15:4; 21:23 (NIV).

"The soothing tongue is a tree of life, but a perverse tongue crushes the spirit. Those who guard their mouths and their tongues keep themselves from calamity. Set a guard over my mouth, LORD; keep watch over the door of my lips." (Psalms 141:3 NIV)

"The tongue has the power of life and death, and those who love it will eat its fruit." (Proverbs 18:21 NIV).

Your life is waiting for more, for better, and it is always great to grow. With one simple tool, things will transform and transition... your tongue has more power than you think.

Shall we begin?

In this book, I emphasize that Faith is real. Faith can be spoken moment by moment, believed moment by moment, and received moment by moment. It takes patience and persistence to accomplish faith.

It is stated in Romans 12:2, *"Be Ye transformed by the renewing of your mind..."*

May I add the renewing of your mind transforms the tongue that translates to you speaking better words that creates better chances.

The Tongue Has Faith: Taste It, Speak It

If you were to come to a better understanding, even a greater understanding, the person who understands this can be as good as made whole as of right now. It gets to the point where it doesn't matter how severe the setback is or how impossible the situation may be, The Past Defeat—YOUR past defeats—at trying to master faith does not matter at this point and time. Faith has worked over and over again. I have known for it to work, because I have watched my father and my mother use it, and I have used it for myself.

Faith works!

Some may ask, "Is it difficult?" Well, anything worth having can be difficult depending on the approach you take when proceeding to obtain what is proclaimed to be yours such as dreams, desires, needs, and wants. Once again (the word of God states), it is according to your belief. Believe it to be hard, difficult, and challenging, and it WILL be hard, difficult, and challenging.

When you think of it as being easy, it shall be easy. The only aspect of this book which may seem a little daunting is no one can do it for you; no one can speak it for you. Failure or Success depends exclusively upon you. It is very important you speak the greatest that can be spoken over your situation and over other situations in your life. Words determine your lifestyle, your beliefs, your attitude, and you as a person.

Jesus made it very clear we will see answers when we believe (Matthew 21:22 following Mark 11:24). In Matthew 9:29, he says, *"According to your faith let it be done to you."* Faith and belief are much more than words or what others think of you, good or bad, right or wrong. Agree with me here when I write that Faith is an attitude.

The chosen words we are going to use will help you by speaking those words over your life, in the form of support to help you and guide you. It is possible you can speak lifestyle into a better existence by realizing the power you have within, the power of speaking, doing, and believing. This belief will help bring about an attitude of <u>I can, I will, I have, and I AM.</u>

When proceeding to read this book, you will come across a symbol along with the words **POWER OF THE TONGUE, ₪ (POTT).** This is where you, as the reader, will repeat the words that follow, insert your name, and meditate on what is being spoken from your very mouth, with your very tongue.

We are here to train the tongue to speak truth, life, joy, wealth, health, love, wisdom, confidence, and many more qualities that will benefit you in living a full life.

Remember, as a man or woman thinks, so is he or she. Why not speak life into your life?

Become aware of how you are feeling, thinking, and speaking at this moment of time in your precious life. How are you viewing yourself as a person? Are you on the mission and assignment that was given to you by the creator, or are you just working to stay alive, to exist? How are you thinking? How are you really thinking?

If your thinking is not healthy, it is possible your speaking is not healthy. Attempt to pause, slow things down, notice, and become aware of what you are thinking and speaking. If it is not healthy, be willing to change. Change now—not at some set future date, but as of right now—at this very present moment.

Monitoring your thoughts constantly may not be necessary. Focus on bringing and speaking about the glorious achievements you want to appear and experience in your life and in the life of others, speaking with ease and not so much with pain.

Take this moment as you read to redirect your thoughts to be as positive and productive as possible. It takes time and effort. It takes making the negativity positive or not accepting the negative at all, sort of like in one ear and out the other.

At this instant, make up your mind you will continue with it tomorrow morning, tomorrow evening, tomorrow night, and from there on. How you start your day is very important, because how you feel then will often set the tone for the entire day ahead of you.

It is entirely possible that you have grown comfortable with fear, doubt, and thoughts about past defeats. These types of thoughts can create tightness in the center of your chest and neck—even on your face. They can sometimes appear as a stomachache or headache.

Do your body a favor and insist on relaxing. You will notice as you relax the chest, relax the shoulders, and relax the thoughts, it is possible to gain amazing precious moments of freedom from your endless search for answers to your many problems, tribulations, or concerns.

Make those mental convoys silent. Eventually, those mental conversations that are not healthy for you will be paused, and life will be back to becoming great again.

₪ POTT: WITH GOD ALL THINGS ARE POSSIBLE

Say the above phrase five times out loud, and then whisper it under your breath. Try writing the phrase on your shower door, your bathroom mirror, and on your car dashboard (with a sticky note). Save it as a reminder on your calendar, and also post it on the home screen of your cell phone. When possible, write the phrase over and over and over for your benefit.

The purpose for this phrase is to transform your life as you speak it off your tongue out of your mouth. This is a way to make sure it becomes a part of you. It doesn't say, "With YOU all things are possible," it clearly states...

"With GOD ALL THINGS ARE POSSIBLE."

All bills are paid; all voids are filled with his true presence, life is restored, and there is a way out of no way being made especially for you.

Take the time to relax and allow the Divine to carry all the heavy loads.

Come to believe, *"With God all things are possible."*

Get to the point that you believe it (insert name here) in spite of yourself.

Again, *"WITH GOD ALL THINGS ARE POSSIBLE."*

Here is the answer you have been waiting for. Don't ever forget it.

Throughout the day or night, do not allow negative thoughts to drift from one worry to another worry or concern.

Treat yourself and do YOURSELF A FAVOR. Immediately stop concerning yourself with doubt, worry, and mental pain from unwelcome thoughts.

Leave it alone and throw it away.

Always bring your attention and your thoughts back to the present. The present is where we are.

"WITH GOD ALL THINGS ARE POSSIBLE."

EVEN THE FUTURE.

Do Not Worry, Speak No Worry

25 "Therefore I tell you, do not worry about your life, what you will eat or drink; or about your body, what you will wear. Is life not more than food, and the body more than clothes? 26 Look at the birds of the air; they do not sow or reap or store away in barns, and yet your heavenly Father feeds them. Are you not much more valuable than they? 27 Can any one of you by worrying add a single hour to your life? 28 And why do you worry about clothes? See how the flowers of the field grow. They do not labor or spin. 29 Yet I tell you that not even Solomon in his entire splendor was dressed like one of these. 30 If that is how God clothes the grass of the field, which is here today and tomorrow is thrown into the fire, will he not much more clothe you—you of little faith? 31 So do not worry, saying, 'What shall we eat?' or 'What shall we drink?' or 'What shall we wear?' 32 For the pagans run after all these things, and your heavenly Father knows that you need them. 33 But seek first his kingdom and his righteousness, and all these things will be given to you as well. 34 Therefore do not worry about tomorrow, for tomorrow will worry about itself. Each day has enough trouble of its own."

(**Footnotes/credited:** Matthew 6:25-34 NIV)

Wow! Look at the proof we do not have to worry! Look at the proof all is going to work out fine. There is an invaluable aid on the road to peace. Simply stop trying to impress others.

Be happy with yourself; however, be willing to grow and help others grow. Be willing to succeed and assist others in achieving success.

Now the question is, "What is success?"

In the world we are living in, success is measured by the clothes, the cars, the houses, and /or the money we obtain… but take a look at a better way to describe success.

What is success in your eyes? What is success to you?

It is stated in the Book of Luke 12:15, *Then he said to them "Watch out! Be on your guard against all kinds of greed; a man's life does not consist in the abundance of his possessions."*

The power of the tongue is more than simple wishes for a better world in a material state. It is an intimate relationship with your creator and his will for you. His will is better than anything you could desire or obtain.

To be in the center of God's will is more fortunate than any material blessing, and being in the center of his will just may include some of the material blessings you have always desired.

It is very important to know your life should not be measured in the collection of material possessions. Success should be acknowledged and applauded but not worshipped; it is great to be obtained but not sought after.

Just imagine or give it a thought that real success consists of way more than riches alone. Riches are what you possess, and wealth is what you are.

Nevertheless, life is going to offer you a ride of ups and downs. It is up to you as a Believer to know all is well. You can only live life one second at a time.

Begin to pay attention to the glories and wonders of God's handiwork. Grasp and hold on to the idea that it is best to spend as much time in the present as possible.

THIS CAN BE AMAZING FOR YOU, AND YES THIS DOES WORK!

Be very patient with yourself. It requires awareness and will pay off as soon as you learn how to speak life into your own situations and into the situations of others. Use your tongue for giving valuable worth to yourself and others.

Believe it or not, it appears to work the exact same way with attitudes. For instance, if you are the type to demonstrate sorrow, it is possible something will happen to justify the sadness.

On the upper hand, do your best to put on a "HAPPY FACE," and believe it or not, one GREAT thing after another will occur to keep you smiling.

Take note of what you are thinking and what you are speaking as good things happen to you. SPEAK them out and acknowledge those good things. Also write them out and keep track of those good things. You'll soon see that belief works, you are grateful for these good things, and you are witnessing proof in small answers that will make you ready to believe for the big ones.

But with all SAID and done, there is a process you must apply no matter what. As you begin to speak what you want into existence, BE PATIENT. Imagine and look forward to the answers that will soon come your way; however, do not persistently look for them. It is possible that focusing on them can ruin the process. Keep your mind clear and the tongue sharp, instead of dwelling on problems and their possible solutions.

Some may put this last, but not least: it is best to read God's Word. What we're attempting to do is to grow in faith by not only reading the word <u>but speaking the word over our lives</u> and into our lives.

Romans 10:17 says, *"Faith cometh by hearing, and hearing by the word of God."*

Therefore, **know** the word, **believe** the word, and **speak** it out loud to yourself and to others.

Speak the word to your situation.

The Power of The Tongue is presented here to facilitate your transformation through the word of God. Before you know it, you will be comprising a new way of thinking, speaking, and believing.

"Old things are passed away; behold, all things are become new." 2 Corinthians 5:17.

Fresh Faith, Fresh Focus, Fresh Fellowship, Fresh Fruit.

Remember Christ states in Matthew 19:26, *"With men this is impossible; but with God ALL THINGS ARE POSSIBLE."*

God can change things. Create the desire to transition to greater, to speak greater, to live greater, to love greater, to search greater, and to desire greater.

Realize you were born; you have purpose; you have freedom to trust and to dream and to speak it OUT LOUD.

God can make a way out of no way, even when a situation seems to be extremely hopeless.

Continue to **speak** greatness, continue to **speak** hope, continue to **speak** favor, and continue to **speak** peace, love, joy, and deliverance.

God can do it. Just because he hasn't done so already is no reason whatsoever to be discouraged. Believe it or not, there is a very good explanation why your prayers have gone unanswered at this moment and time.

Refer to James 1:6 where it is stated we are to *"ask in faith, nothing wavering."* If we do waver, it goes to show in verse 7, *"let not that man think that he shall receive any thing of the Lord."*

Think about this for a minute or two. Who among us can say we have not wavered? We waver in our faith because we ask God to do something, but instead of waiting for him to complete the task or journey ahead, we become impatient and do it ourselves.

Sometimes it is better to Give up the burden!

Leave it in his Hands!

Stop trying so hard to make it happen!

"Do not worry" is to grow stronger in your faith. It is of no benefit to worry all while trying your best to maintain and operate in faith. This is where the value of growth takes place, and the power of speaking specifically in faith is a benefit that produces blessing after blessing after blessing.

Growth; Expanding My Taste Buds

"Don't become like people of this world, instead, change the way you think. Then you will always be able to determine what God really wants—what is good, pleasing, and perfect." (Romans 12:2)

₪ (POTT): Father God, it is by your mercy and Grace that I am able to stand before you today and change my way of thinking and speaking. Father God, because I AM WILLING to change the way I think, I know it will change the way I act. Therefore, from this day forward Father God, I (<u>say name here</u>) am not like people of this world. Instead, I (<u>say name here</u>) change the way I think and speak, and now I am able to determine what God really wants for me; God wants what is good for me; God wants what is pleasing for me; and God wants what is perfect for me, according to Romans 12:2. Therefore I receive this.

The above statement is spoken to acknowledge, as a person, you are willing to grow, you are ready to grow, and you know growth is available to you as of right now. It may seem like the world sometimes makes growth impossible; however, what you need to know about growth is it requires obedience and patience with yourself as well as with others.

When you decide you are ready to grow, change is going to come. What are you going to do to make this transition possible?

Reciting scripture and memorizing mottos and quotes is a start. The goal is to live out the scripture, experiencing and accepting the truths that are written. You should speak scripture with your mouth, but it is better when you put it in your heart.

With all growth, there will be growing pains.

Wait...you mean to tell me there is pain involved?

Growing pains will help you understand change is coming and needs to be accepted.

Growing pains make room for the better quality of life you will be rewarded with when you trust in the higher power, creating and speaking new thoughts and experiencing new, stronger faith that will put your mind be at ease.

Growing pains result in accepting you simply might not get what you desire when you want it. But with patience, practice, and understanding, it will be on time.

While growing, it is highly recommended you practice gratitude as you witness and observe smallest of answers which will make it easier for you to believe for the big answers which you have prayed and hoped for.

Growth takes place in the mind which helps in turn with the language and words that are spoken by the believer. <u>Words</u> that are spoken and meditated on help transform the attitude of the one who is searching and being receptive to change.

Attitude is very important when believing and training the tongue. Besides speaking great and having your wants and desires at the forefront of your mind, intentions of the believer's attitude toward God and his power is the true developer.

Effective living and believing begins with the right attitude toward God. Respect for the word of God should characterize one's attitude toward God and others.

No matter where you are in life, you are there by the grace of God. When people speak of you, and when you speak of others, use the tongue as the heart of the conversation. Be at ease, and only speak what is necessary.

Words are very valuable, so make your mouth the conversation piece that is priceless.

When a lyricist writes a song, he or she is doing their best to get a point across, such as love, joy, a lost, or a gain. Words have to make sense to move the audience if the song is created for a purpose. How about using this as an example when you are engaged in conversations throughout your day?

As I was growing up, my father and mother had several friends who were in business for themselves, and many were builders of some sort. It always amazed me that the builder had to first lay the foundation—normally made of steel, concrete, or maybe even stone, and the purpose of the foundation was to hold a house together from underneath. A builder who has wisdom concerning his craft knows to build the foundation on rock, something that is very reliable and steady.

You can take the above example and advise people that for the very same reason, they need to build their heart-felts, their conversations about each other, and their heart's desires and dreams upon a strong foundation—the promises of God.

Build your life and conversations on the Rock—God Almighty. The result of your conversations will be dependable and solid.

You can always rely on God and his very own word, simply because he is the one who always tells what is true. It is beneficial to have conversations which follow a good plan such as the ones found in God's very own word.

There are many people, young, old, wealthy, and poor who don't follow the best plan on building their power through the tongue. There are many who do not know about the instructions God gives us in the Bible for building our lives by speaking and believing. There are many who know about the Bible but decide to ignore it.

There are many warnings included in the Bible concerning people who decide to build their lives on unstable foundations. Some have built their foundation on sand, an example of speaking negatively into their own lives and the lives of others. Some examples include: "This is too hard. That would never happen to me. It is too good to be true."

Many people speak the poison of nonexistence into their lives. Their very own words are a thief to the dreams and desires that could possibly come true. Perhaps this is a result of their being accustomed to speaking negatively and unproductively for so long they don't realize they are building their foundation on sand. They take it upon themselves to decide what is correct and what is incorrect, speaking and meditating on what they believe in their own minds.

When people speak without guidance on certain matters, especially without the guidance of God, their lives can take a turn for the worse. When their foundation isn't stable, their lives can start to fall apart and take a downward turn.

Your very own tongue is the architect for building your life. Know the word of God and his plan for you which has everything you need, including a safety plan. When followed and taken seriously and faithfully, his Word will keep you from speaking all kinds of danger, and it is even available to show you the very way out of adverse situations.

The question is, does your foundation have a crack in it?

Are you speaking with a solid foundation?

Do your best daily to "make a note of it." Keep a journal in which you take the time to write out the way you intend for things to go in your life and in the lives of others.

Keep in mind it is very important to consider positive word play. This is your life! Always keep the best options at the forefront of your thoughts and your desires.

Record in your notebook or on your tablet your answers to life's important questions.

Refer to scripture for the answer and the solution.

Once you find the scripture that refers to your situation or concern, remember to read the given promise out loud to yourself daily or as much as needed until it becomes your truth.

For instance, there may come a time when you are tired, or when you feel like nothing is working the way you planned; a time you may feel everything you are doing amounts to nothing, and your purpose has failed. but there is hope in Jeremiah 29:11.

₪ POTT: For I know the plans I have for you,

(insert name here), declares the Lord, "plans to prosper you and not to harm you, plans to give you hope and a future."

Most of the time, it is thought patterns which train the tongue to speak. Shall you decide to journal, speak out loud about what you want to do, where you want to go, and what foundation you will build to get there.

Use your tongue to build your house (your life) on solid foundation, because it is very important that the foundation you build has the ability to weather the storm. Therefore, it is better to build your life on the solid Rock of God and his Word than with your own emotions.

A question to ask oneself is: How am I building my life around my speech and my devotion with the word of God?

Your knowledge and belief of scripture is the concrete structure which will support you in building a solid foundation.

Your speech will build from wisdom, and wisdom is gained from knowing, loving, obeying God, and applying the knowledge to speak Godly decisions.

Several Ways to Build the Tongue

Take time out of your life for a day of observation. Perhaps ride the bus instead of driving, so you have opportunities to listen to conversations—listen to their language and their thought patterns.

When the people you see the most or converse with daily have a huge influence in your life and an influence on the progression in your life, pay attention to how their speech and tongue aerobics are affecting you.

Are you aware of the way you are thinking or speaking?

How is your speech enhancing their life?

In life, there are always more ways to improve. Take a look at the following ways to help mature and build the tongue.

Study and Learn the Bible

What is the purpose of having a weapon if you are not taking the time necessary to figure out how to use it effectively?

Many of you most likely have books sitting in your home, in your office, and downloaded on your device you use daily; however, they are just laying around storing dust or taking up space. Like many books in life we purchase, you get the most out of them by picking them up, studying them, and learning the lessons they teach.

In the world, there is so much available to study. There are history books which teach you about experiences from thousands of years ago. There is the Owner's Manual when you purchase a brand-new vehicle or a new computer. Many will take the time to study this type of literature.

The point I am making is, you get the most out of what you study, apply the principles, and put these principles into practice daily. One should especially read the Bible, which is an instruction manual and owner's manual for life, written by God Himself.

"Take in account that all scripture is given by God and is useful for our teaching and for showing us what is wrong in their lives and how to correct our wrongs for a better life, a heaven on earth life, a full life. It is useful for correcting faults and teaching how to live right. Using the scriptures, the person who serves God will be ready and will have everything he needs to do every good work." (2 Timothy 3:16-17, ICB)

Reassure yourself that an important step to training the tongue is making time to read and think about the

Word of God everyday as your guide, your joy, your peace, and your security.

Think about this when you open your Bible to read it: you are entering into the very presence of God, and when you allow him the chance, he is going to speak to you. It is an opportunity for you to take upon his language and his teachings which will reveal understanding to you.

The time you spend studying the Bible is valuable, as you are now walking and talking with God. Make it a commitment to memorize God's Word. Let it roll off your tongue to pour into your life and the life of others. Take the time to store it away in your heart and in your mind.

God's Word is treasure far more valuable than anything you can own.

His word will keep you from sin (Psalm 119:11).

His word is capable of filling your heart with joy (Jeremiah 15:16).

And as mentioned earlier, to give you peace (Psalm 85:8), prepare you to do good (2 Timothy 3:16-17), and provide you power in Prayer (John 15:7).

Theodore Roosevelt (1859-1919) once stated: *"Knowledge of the Bible is worth more than a college education."*

Know Truth, Speak Truth, Follow Truth

₪ **POTT: I, (<u>insert name here</u>), "Trust Also In Him; He Shall Bring It To Pass." Psalm 37:5**

Know Truth.

What you do not know is what you are not accountable for. What you DO know holds you accountable to do better.

I was in the company of an associate who is known for speaking his mind. He would say things like, "I am so tired, and this body is more than worn out." He would always exaggerate about the fact that he has tried faith, and he has spent several hours praying hard. And with all the praying, he still did not seem to gain any answered prayers.

Wow, praying HARD!!! Many have and still are suffering from this. "Let's pray hard so we can be heard, and answers will come," is what they believe.

Know Truth.

Try this for the next day or so. Believe and know right at this moment tomorrow morning the Lord will allow the sun to exist and allow light upon the earth. Believe it will rise once again.

Now take a deep breath, which was easy to do and believe. There should have been no type of tension to have believed the sun will come and go as usual or to take a deep breath. You should have just simply and calmly accepted it.

The very same feeling of belief in the knowing of the word, which helps you speak to yourself in the time of trouble and in the time of doubt, will bring success with all the other things which you desire.

Do your best to speak and be light-hearted and unconcerned when talking and speaking with God about how you feel and about the burden you are carrying.

Speak to the burden with the word of God and the power he has equipped you with through him. You will notice the burden will astonishingly and magnificently be lifted, no matter how long you have carried it. Know it. Jesus has said this to you in (Matthew 21:22).

There are people who will give a million dollars to be able to release their faith. True Faith is priceless.

Faith is powerful—it can change your thinking, which can change your speaking. There is enough power in faith to take away worries and concerns about having enough money to meet the bills.

Faith casts out fear toward the future. Speaking in faith over all your situations has the power to place you in front and above the crowd which prepares you to soar above the clouds.

It doesn't take money to have faith. It takes the power of the word of God, and it takes chance—a chance to know the abundant life of faith, and you can and will experience the richest and most powerful experiences as the wealthiest people on earth.

It is as simple as speaking your life into existence, creating faith. This is the best way to see results, and always remember it requires alertness of one's speech and word choice.

You must pay attention to your tongue because your thoughts follow what you speak and vice versa. Remain calm and balanced at all times when speaking about desires (Matthew 21:21). Speak and act as if you already possess that which you seek (Mark 11:24).

Learn not to speak negative; learn not to pray hard. Instead, speak positive, know faith, pray easy. "*God knows the very thought of your heart*" (Hebrews 4:12) and is very aware of every one of your needs (Matthew 6:8).

Concern is the very cousin of doubt, and doubt is what keeps you from seeing answers (James 1:6). Speak in

Prayer with a light heart. It should be evident by now it does not work the other way around.

Speak well, no matter how terrible or how heavy the burden may seem to you. Speak well, because the answer is on the way. Display faith in your daily tongue (speech), and your speaking of faith will not go unrewarded. Speak Trust.

Care for Your Tongue, and Use It in the Right Way

"Do not let any part of your body become an instrument of evil to serve sin..." This is what the apostle Paul wrote in Romans 6:13, NLT.

The main purpose of training the tongue, focusing on monitoring your choice of words towards concerns and circumstances, is to influence the inner mind through suggestion. It is something you do every day, which is speaking.

The purpose of training the tongue is to speak at your peak as much as possible to aid as a self-therapy and help you reach your goals. This is where I would suggest self-talk. To protect yourself from harm, self-talk may be necessary.

Everyone you tell your ideas or dreams or desires to may not agree with what you're telling them at the moment, or they may not have the faith it takes to see your desires come to pass. Look at self-talk as a way you treat yourself.

When you're talking to yourself in a mirror or in the car, on a jog or wherever it sees fit for you, talk with yourself about setting your goals and reaching them. Anyone with problems or concerned with decisions which need to be made usually wants the solution to come quick and be rid of the problem(s) as quickly as possible. Narrow your situation to a simple solution.

Once you have had your self-talk, always find the scripture that supports your situation which will allow you to live instead of just exist. It is possible the answers will come to you in an astonishing short time when you employ verbal enhancement with given scripture along with belief.

It is proven in scripture that you have been given the power to be healed. The relief you are health, happiness, and your best can be reached through your very own efforts. Spend the time to know yourself and know self-knowledge is essential. Welcome in your self-talk and be a great listener.

Sing With That Tongue

Growing up, I was blessed that my father's side of the family would sing, and they would sing songs that were filled with praise. Each member had such a great voice, and it was truly amazing.

Speaking the word of God is a healing within itself. Have you considered singing your way into the joy and peace you desire? There are plenty of beautiful songs that declare, "You were made to succeed, and you were made to worship."

"Sing psalms, hymns and spiritual songs with gratitude in your hearts to God." (Colossians 3:16)

Signify Prayer With Your Tongue

1 Thessalonians 5:17 in the Bible tells us to *"pray and to pray continually."*

Use your tongue to speak to God, not always to others about the need or the situation.

Tell God what you are in need of and thank him in advance for all he has done. (Philippians 4:6)

"Don't worry about anything, no matter what pray about everything."

Use that very tongue to pray for yourself and to pray for others, pray for your family, and keep in prayer the things that worry you or concern you.

For whom he is, Pray to God, for all he has done, pray to God.

Learn to take the spotlight off of you and thank him for the food you consume, the clothes you wear, your very home, even thank him for the rain and the sunshine. Thank him for the good, the bad, and the better.

Many people talk to God but fail at listening for him to respond. Prayer is a two-way conversation between you and him, which is two people who have love for each other.

Tongue Tithes

There may be times when your words are your bond. It is all you have—nothing more and nothing less.

There may come a time in your life when you realize money does not buy everything you desire… so, what now?

Perhaps, you may realize your possessions in this life are short-lived. Possessions can easily be stolen or damaged or destroyed by time and decay.

You may think a rich man or woman could simply go out and buy whatever he feels will conquer and make him/her joyful and at peace, but in the times we live in, an entire fortune can be made and lost in merely a moment.

We are warned in the Bible specifically against putting our trust in money or earthly possessions. According to Matthew 6:19-21…

"Do not store up for yourselves treasures on earth, where moth and rust destroy, and where thieves break in and steal. But store up for yourselves treasures in heaven, where moth and rust do not destroy, and where thieves do not break in and steal. For where your treasure is, there your heart will be also."

This does not mean there is something evil about earning money or owning material things. The importance is where you allow your heart to be and what you are allowing your tongue to speak concerning your priorities.

How do you allow your tongue to speak about money? An easy way to look at it is like this—the father reminded us our DAILY BREAD is what is needed.

"For we brought nothing into his world, and we can take nothing out of it. But if we have food and clothing, we will be content with that. Those who want to get rich fall into temptation and a trap and into many foolish and harmful desires that plunge people into ruin and destruction. For the love of money is a root of all of kinds of evil. Some people, eager for money, have wandered from the faith and pierced themselves with many griefs." (1 Timothy 6:10).

When you know the tongue is capable of taking everything you speak to yourself literally, you will want to word your conversations the way you really mean.

It takes time and practice to establish the truth and faith to speak your wants and desires into existence.

Reword your thoughts and suggestions in a way that is going to benefit your life.

Reword the subject matter so that the objective is to push you forward and closer to your desired destiny.

Redirect your speaking for the best.

₪ **POTT: I, (insert name here), am allowing myself to speak greatness into my life one sentence at a time.**

How are you allowing yourself to speak right before you see answers to prayer?

How do you speak when you are in a state of receiving?

Don't be afraid to be happy and speak happiness. This is very important. Many wonderful things will come to take place as you speak.

Be glad about what is to come, do not be like the soul who speaks in doubt.

The power used by the tongue when performed regularly will work. You must decide whether it is worth the effort.

You have to decide whether you are content to live a full life or half a life.

Engaging Self-Talk That Satisfies

₪POTT: I, (insert name here), am either going to make it or I'm not.

Let's take the time to become aware of what works with speaking greatness and truth into your life and the lives of others. We both know it gives you hope and an expectation of the greatness to come as well as a chance to grow.

Suggestions of using the tongue to speak and bring power and enlighten your awareness of speaking the truth of the scripture is great; however, there are certain methods which will help the process seem natural.

The power of the tongue can be a great advantage when you engage in self-talk. You will find self-talk will help you become more relaxed during your daily life. Who is a better cheerleader or motivator than yourself? You know what you desire, you know what you want and how you expect to get it done, and where you would like for life to take you.

For instance, say you are tired at the beginning or the end of the day, and you must continue because the day is full of expectations of yourself and others who are counting on you. A few moments of self-talk with suggestions of speaking positive about your situation, circumstance, or responsibility can refresh you and bring about feelings targeted toward vitality.

When you have learned how to produce the right kind of self-talk, you'll be able to shut off negativity as well as negative talk from others, a real asset to your life.

Self-talk has a purpose. It will reassure you that by trusting the positive, you will attract positive reactions, solutions, and results.

Self-talk can be very helpful in learning to study poems and Bible verses which help you realize the value of speaking and reciting encouraging literature. You are a good enough subject to concentrate on the ability to speak performance, speak progression, and experience change through the power of the tongue.

When you intend to open the mouth and engage in self-talk, concentrate on the abilities you have to offer the world and what you have to give. You deserve to verbalize constructive talk, so in return, you will receive more strength for your mind and body which will increase your confidence.

When engaged in self-talk, do not speak doubt over yourself. Learn to speak and delight over the amazing strengths you have now. Be thankful they are yours to keep and to share with others. Learn to verbally congratulate yourself and pat yourself on the back for all you have accomplished this far in life but leave room for what is to come.

In self-talk, speak positive about the things that make you happy and build yourself up.

Remain lively of the heart, speak happiness into the thought, narrate strong of the mind, and sound in being.

Hold a mental vision of what you are speaking, get a feeling of what you are speaking, and experience it.

Hear yourself speaking, bring out the details with your speech, be very vivid with your words, and develop your hearing for your voice by listening to whatever positive words being said.

With a modest practice, you will find yourself automatically using the tongue to bring about life's positive episodes. You may find yourself speaking your worries away, your doubts away, and bringing in life and success to you scene by scene, self-talk by self-talk.

In all situations, speak into the situation with a positive, creative force. You may even be able to go back and verbally reconstruct past events, turning the negative experience into a more positive one.

Always keep in mind that with self-talk, you are living the experience verbally, so speak to yourself as the most positive participant you can be or become.

Self-talk is accomplished more ways than one. You have more than enough equipment around you than you know to enhance your self-talk. If you own a cell phone which has a recorder programmed on the device, or if you have a tape recorder, consider recording your self-talk.

Incorporate the verbal motivation needed for you day by day or hour by hour, whatever your preference or need is at the time. Record your personal self-motivation speech, play it over and over to yourself, and listen and feel the power of the tongue.

I personally have a self-talk I listen to in the morning and at night as I sleep. I was fortunate at the time to have an associate with a recording studio who allowed me to record my self-talk so I could have it with me at all times.

You can record your very own voice or have someone else do this for you. Just make sure when you are recording, express through your voice how you are feeling. Speak with excitement and confidence about the greater good that is to come concerning the circumstance you are facing or the result of success you are expecting.

When you listen to your self-talk, make sure to smile, and use the most positive expression that will help you experience the joy of knowing this self-talk is now the new enhancement to a life of achievements and grand accomplishments. Be creative with your self-talk recordings. Use music and sound that make your inspiration more realistic.

Self-talk is self-betterment. Don't worry about overdoing it. Remember to be kind and speak well to yourself.

Speaking life to yourself is real freedom of speech!!!

₪ **POTT: God created me, (insert name here), with a purpose for life. I have life.**

Tongue Material

Most everyone has wondered or wanted to know about the future. I think if we knew the future by every detail, we would feel our decisions would be easier, and life would be grand.

Some of us walk a very thin line in life that is weighed between the possible and what is described as impossible. When you take time to sit and reevaluate your life, pray and believe you are closer to living a magnificent life free from doubt and terror.

I feel this is why I was led to do such a book on the Power of the Tongue, because one word or phrase you speak can change an entire situation.

One of the best ways in the world to influence yourself and others is by the power of speaking. Notice and evaluate the tongue. Notice how a fall of the tongue influences your believing and affects your subconscious mind.

Verbal treatment is self-treatment. Most people speak without realizing the control they have in their words. Words can produce and cause expectations of good or bad results in one's life. A negative conversation can intensify an existing negative attitude, along with resulting darkened outlooks.

Take the time to notice what I like to call "Verbal Stones." Verbal stones are dangerous and can cause you to fail at what is achievable.

Here are some examples:

I CAN'T instead of the great defining I CAN, or I WILL.

When I hear others speak of the words I CAN'T, I take upon the meaning that I CAN'T is somewhat saying: "I do not want to try this, because I am afraid I will fail or there is a possibility of failure."

I CAN'T is the cousin of doubt and the neighbor of misery.

A very popular Verbal Stone is simply saying I'LL TRY. This is merely another way of saying you most likely will not succeed. Stay away from those VERBAL STONES that are causing doubt and misleading your life.

Immaturity does not always come in the way a person acts—it can come in the form of verbal lack. Verbal lack is speaking with an immature basis, using absolutes like always and never.

For example, "I always have bad days," or "Nothing good ever happens to me." It is possible that as you speak it, you will live it. Verbal lack can cause a person to feel or become depressed.

"I know they will not like my idea," kind of thinking makes for a verbal fulfilling prophecy. When a person has already acknowledged in their mind something is not right, or no one will agree, most likely when given the chance to speak about it, they will.

When you think thoughts of not feeling good all the time or thoughts of depression or self-lack all the time, normally you won't expect good things to happen in your life of the life of others.

On a better note, positive thoughts play a huge part in exercising the power of the tongue. Thinking positive thoughts and speaking positive words will help you be more effective in your life.

What you allow to enter your mind each and every day will determine and conduct the conversations that impact where you are heading in life and how quickly you get there.

Thoughts are very real—they carry over to helpful words or verbal stones. They are so real, they impact how you feel, speak, and behave. Speaking negatively or speaking in doubt is like pollution to the body.

When you are not receiving the results you desire, it is important to learn from your very own mouth. How are you speaking about your situation? Are you speaking to your situation in a balanced and positive way? If not, it looks as if you have homework to do.

Make it an assignment to speak with life, love, and power. Make it a point to give your conversation more balance and optimism. Get rid of the verbal turbulence that holds you back from achieving the goals you desire. Always search and surround yourself with positive people. Positive people have the desire to speak positive.

Look at your life and evaluate your surroundings. What kind of people are you around? Does the crowd of people you hang with speak in an uplifting way? Do they believe in you and your dreams, or are they constantly speaking down and burying your ideas, desires, and hopes?

Take the time to list the top seven people you spend time with. Evaluate and make sure it is an enhancing group. Surround yourself and be one of the people of the group who have an uplifting spirit that will breathe hope into your plans. Always consider that "Iron sharpens Iron."

Let's Talk, Tongue IQ

₪ (POTT): "Now to him is able to do immeasurably more than all we ask or imagine, according to his power that is work within us, to him be glory in the church and in Christ Jesus throughout all generations, for ever and ever!" (Ephesians 3:20-21)

Everyone's life is full of stories, some of us have many to tell, and many of us have listened to a great deal of stories this far in our lives, but what do those stories consist of? Are they stories that inspire, or are they stories that hinder you from believing in what is possible?

It is one thing to listen to immature speaking; however, speaking immaturely or speaking without faith and belief shows that one has not grown higher in his or her knowledge that the very power of their tongue holds the key to what is going to happen and how it will come about.

When you are always speaking negatively and with doubt, sooner or later your subconscious mind will confirm what you are saying. With the tongue, the acceptance of words has the power to close and open doors. I have to continue to repeat this throughout the book because it is very important to know.

"Finally, brethren, whatever is honorable, whatever is right, whatever is pure, whatever is lovely, whatever is of good repute, if there is any excellence and if there is anything worthy of praise, let your mind dwell on these things." (Philippians 4:8)

Your state of mind has tremendous control over how you speak. A committed tongue is powerful and structured with material to promote growth.

I am a big fan of poetry and inspirational quotes. I feel everyone should have quotes and scripture visible in their homes, offices, and gyms reminding us of God's promises to his children, and enlightenment from other authors and artists is just icing on the cake.

"Let's Talk" points out that no matter what we ask for, what we think we need, or what our desires are, we have a heavenly Father who knows all before we can even ask of him. He will give to his children; he will provide for you. However, you must be willing and ready to receive.

In "Let's Talk," I will provide scriptures that you are advised to study, believe, and recite to yourself—out loud—or post where the scripture is visible. Allow the promises of God to have meaning as well as a personal and affectionate feeling toward your circumstances and situations.

"Let's Talk" is based on Biblical Truth, truth that is better for tongue than anything you could speak or recite. Speaking faith makes a big difference. Make sure your faith-speaking and reciting results in action. Always be alert to ways you are verbally putting your faith to work. Be certain you not only talk the Gospel and the inspirational poems and quotes, but you also walk it.

Successfully speaking over your adversaries will produce maturity and strong character. Do not make it a habit to resist trials and tribulations as they come. Use this very tongue to pray for wisdom about your concern, circumstance, or matter, and believe God will provide all you need to stand. He will give you patience and keep you stronger than you can imagine.

We are held accountable for how we use our tongue. We should speak generously toward others with our words and towards ourselves as well. Should you desire to live your life as a great achiever, should you desire to overcome the tribulations in your life and soar to take lead of the days when fate conspires to see you do great things with your life, should you desire to live a full life, remember it starts in your speaking. With your mouth, you have the path to magnitude.

I invite you to **TALK IT OUT** and **SPEAK IT OUT**. Here it is personalized for you: Let's see the Power in Your Tongue.

"One who has any faith in God should be ashamed to worry about anything whatsoever."

Mahatama Gandhi

₪ (POTT): I, <u>(insert name here)</u>, "Trust in the LORD with all my heart and I lean not on my own understanding; in all my ways I acknowledge him, and he will make my paths straight," according to Proverbs 3:5-6.

₪ (POTT): "God is my, (insert name here), refuge and strength, and my ever-present help in trouble. Therefore I, (insert name here), will not fear," according to Proverbs 46:1-2.

₪ (POTT): "For God did not give me, (insert name here), the spirit of timidity, but a spirit of power, love and of self-discipline," according to 2 Timothy 1:7.

₪ (POTT): "Because I, (insert name here), have set the LORD always before me. Because he is my right hand, I, (insert name here), will not be shaken," according to Psalm 16:8.

₪ (POTT): "I, (insert name here), cast my cares on the Lord and he will sustain me, he will never let the righteous fall," according to Psalm 55:22.

₪ (POTT): "I, (insert name here), cast all my anxiety on him because he cares for me," according to 1 Peter 5:7.

₪ (POTT): "Let the words of my, (insert name here), mouth, and the meditation of my heart, be acceptable in thy sight, O Lord my strength and redeemer," according to Psalm 19:14.

₪ (POTT): "As for God, his way is perfect: the word of the Lord is: he is a buckler to all those who trust him," according to Psalm 18:30.

₪ (POTT): "The Lord is my, (insert name here), rock, my fortress, and my deliverer; my strength, in whom I trust; my buckler, and the horn of my salvation, and my high tower," according to Psalm 18:2.

₪ (POTT): "The Lord is my, (insert name here), Shepherd, I shall not want," according to Psalm 23:1.

₪ (POTT): "The Lord is my light and my, (insert name here), light and salvation; whom shall I fear? The Lord is the strength of my life; of whom shall I be afraid," according to Psalm 27:1.

₪ (POTT): "In everything I, (insert name here), will give thanks," according to 1 Thessalonians 5:18.

"Be strong in the Lord and the power of his might," according to Ephesians 6:10.

The scriptures listed in this book are nuggets of truth and power. God has many more to offer in his word. You will be amazed to see this process working in your life once you personalize the scripture with your name and the names of your family members, friends, and loved ones.

God has power, and he can express his power through you. It is wonderful that he left the word for us to rely on, so we do not have to be intimidated by anyone. All we have to do is speak forth HIS word as he gives it to you.

When you are in the word of God, do not study just to please man—focus on pleasing God. Search your very own heart, and pray for strength to seek his word, live it, and receive from it.

Keep in mind your committed tongue is powerful, and when structured with appropriate material, it will promote growth.

You are Tongue IQ at its best.

Building a Tower with the Tongue

It is amazing how we have access to such a remarkable and powerful tool. We have complete ownership to what is capable of making our life whole and complete when allowed—God's Truth—his word.

In Genesis 11:4, The Tower of Babel was an amazing achievement, a remarkable wonder of the world. However, it was a monument to the people for their desires and requirements instead of what God desired.

Often in this day and age, we as people, we as seekers, we as believers, often build monuments to and for ourselves, examples of the modern-day tower. Examples of modern-day towers are expensive clothes, a big house, fancy vehicles, and an important (prestigious) job.

Do not take it in the wrong way—these are not wrong in themselves—only when we use them to give ourselves identity and make ourselves feel more worthy than other people. These towers can steal or take God's most precious and VIP spots in our lives.

The good news is, we are liberated to expand in many areas of life; however, we are not free if we have replaced God with these material things.

Speaking and standing on the word of God will bring such material blessings. Living the word of God and training the tongue results in spiritual growth which is very simple when you read the scriptures that refer to all of what you desire coming together for those who...

"Seek ye first the kingdom of God and his righteousness; and all these things shall be added unto you." (Matthew 6:33)

At all times, speak with love, joy, peace and understanding. Incorporating these expressions into your dialogue will result in what is best for you and other people. It leaves out room for negativity, self-doubt, and bashing, which in turn leads to less being accomplished and more difficulty as your new possession.

God may be trying to lead you to a place of superior service and effectiveness for him. Don't allow the comfort of your present way of talking or thinking make you miss God's plan for you by speaking less of yourselves or less of others. It starts in your mind and out through your mouth. Make what comes out of your mouth of benefit to yourself and others, not a hindrance to yourself and others.

When attempting to achieve goals and keep faith, speak great over yourself and the situation you are facing. Say to yourself daily...

"IF GOD IS FOR ME, THEN WHO CAN BE AGAINST ME." (Romans 8:31).

When you are a child of the Most-High God, this promise belongs to you. Claim it, accept it, agree with it, live it, and help others do the same.

"ACCORDING TO YOUR FAITH BE IT UNTO YOU." (Matthew 9:29)

Reader, it is necessary for me to say to you from experience when you are having difficulties in life and are looking for answers, there is a secure way to deal with these matters. When you take a burden to the Lord, how soon and in what manner for yourself would you like to see an answer?

Let's think about this here. If you are anything like people who are looking and praying for answers, you would most likely say, "immediately," and you would also most likely want the answer to be as easy as possible to retrieve.

I think, for the most part, we all have a tendency to be this way. Instead of a person in the Bible or a person who is living today, we want what we want when we want it, and at the most, we want it now.

When we take the time to seek our answers or a particular something through prayer, we are in a rush to get it right now, with as little liability on our part as possible.

It is very different with other things. For example, if we wish to play the trumpet or become a professional writer or learn to sing well, we accept the fact that it takes time and practice to do these things we set out to achieve. Practice is the first necessity of them all, which is something we all understand.

Adopt the same understanding when it comes to mastering the power of the tongue, including the meanings to the words we speak and the prayers we pray.

Calmness, confidence, and a state of believing can make all the difference as to whether or not you will see answers to what you are most concerned about or what you are taking to God.

In 2 Peter 1:5-7, there is a list of seven characteristics God wants us to add to our lives. To build up our faith, Paul advises us to add these qualities to our faith: goodness, knowledge, self-control, perseverance, godliness, mutual affection, and above all, Love. If these are qualities you are lacking, simply work to possess these qualities in increasing measures.

Know at any place and time in your life, God is ready and able to present miracles. Imagine the joy you would feel when you speak these miracles before they exist in the physical.

Verbally call upon the blessings you desire. Verbally speak life's powerful anointing and blessings over your life and the lives of others. Commit to a daily practice of claiming your way to hope, faith, newness, overflow, health, joy, and the desires that will make and keep your life worth living.

If you feel you need a miracle in your life, always define what that one thing is and how it is going to be of benefit to not only you, but to others. For instance, if you are seeking miracles daily, define what a miracle is to you. If a miracle is defined as "that thing or something so complex that only God can accomplish it," then make sure you highlight the area of your life that is most in need of a miracle and how this miracle compares to your faith of this miracle being obtained with God.

Are you speaking this miracle into existence? Have you compared these miracles to the miracles of the stories in the Bible where God has performed miracle after miracle time and time again?

In Genesis 18:14, The Lord said to Abraham, *"Is anything too hard for the Lord?"*

It is told in the Bible Abraham fathered Isaac at age one hundred. Moving on to more miracles, consider in 2 Kings 3:18, when Elisha told Joram and his thirsty troops God was going to fill the valley with water. Elisha assured the king, *"This is an easy thing in the eyes of the Lord."* The very next morning, water came. *"For no word from God will ever fail,"* the angel told Mary according to Luke 1:37. And a virgin gave birth to a savior.

So, I say to ask this: What challenge in your life seems too big for you to speak over and give it life with the word of God? What challenge is too big for anyone but God?

Take the time to search the Bible and write your name by the stories that relate to you and your situation. Let this be your testimony of self-assurance in God's ability to do the impossible in your life as well as in the lives of others. Even though you may ask God to do something FOR you, consider he normally wants to do something IN you.

Your knowledge of knowing what God is capable of doing extends the invitation of what he is going to do for you. Expect the miracle, speak the miracle, and it shall come to pass.

It's in the Power of Your Tongue.

Verbal Visions

₪ (POTT): "With men this is impossible; but with God all things are possible." (Matthew 19:26)

There are many comforting and uplifting verses in God's written word, but I wonder if you'll be in agreement with me that Matthew 19:26 is one of the most reassuring and supportive, especially when we have wants, needs and desires to be met:

With God all things are possible.

ALL things!

That takes in a lot, but Jesus said it, and Jesus speaks the truth. All things are possible with God! That means we can see answers not only to miniature problems but to those which require miracles as well. Even unsaid and unspoken requests can become reality. That innermost, intimate desire—that one desire we hesitate to even share with close friends and almost dare not hope for, CAN be fulfilled, praise the Lord.

EVERYTHING is possible!

If we have a physical problem, he can make us whole. He can assemble the cells and cause a heart or anything else to become absolutely faultless and perfect. It doesn't matter whether or not the doctors or any type of medical science has the solution, he can make all things right. There could have been an infirmity which has burdened you or someone you have known for years. With his power and your faith, it can be made all right.

In some cases, success may have eluded you for years. You may have known only heartaches and failure all your life. This, too, can change—and it can change overnight—for with GOD, ALL things are possible.

This is true for your concerns about financial needs, even if life has always been a week-to-week existence, and you seem to see no way out. That's all right. Literally, it is ALL RIGHT for God, who will make a way where there is none.

All things are possible with GOD.

On the road to answered desires and answered prayer, it is important to believe all things are possible with God. This is perhaps the first and the most essential step.

When our hearts are filled with the knowledge of this 'all-encompassing' fact, we then have a better chance to believe for our own particular requests. And Jesus said (Matthew 21:22), *"And all things, whatsoever ye shall ask in prayer, believing, ye shall receive."*

If for years, however, we have known defeat and discouragement, it can be extremely difficult to believe and '**release faith**' verbally. Drained of confidence and enthusiasm, even taking the first step can seem overwhelming. Take the first step, though, and the road to victory will become increasingly easier.

Okay, let's review what was established in the beginning of this book; try this if you have not already: Primarily, make several signs with paper, note cards, write on memo boards, or chalk boards saying,

WITH GOD ALL THINGS ARE POSSIBLE.

Place them where you'll be sure to see them often: on the bathroom mirror, the dashboard of the car, on the cover of your Bible. What we want to do is to hold that thought constantly before our minds.

Repeat the words often and say it with conviction:

With God ALL things are possible!

Feel what you are saying. Close your eyes, see what you want, and imagine yourself with it; experience the emotion of receiving the blessing at hand. It is even better to write it over and over and post the blessing where you can read it and store it in your memory every day. This is a way to create a gateway to make it become a part of you. Soon you will come to believe it "in spite of yourself." Always speak it!!

How do you use the tongue in a truthful approach, an approach that produces a formation of living and letting go? Nothing great can take place if you do not have faith, so start with your way of speaking. Verbalize in such a way that you refuse to believe it could go wrong; speak in such a way that whatever is holding you back has to come to a close; speak in such a way that you can speak to the mountain and it uproots and moves.

"For verily I say unto you, That whosoever shall say unto this mountain, Be thou removed, and be..." (Mark 11:23)

Jesus said we should **speak to the mountain**, or the problem. It is very important you not only speak to your mountain, know your mountain. Your mountain is anything and everything that is slowing you down. It is anything that is impeding your progress in the kingdom of God, whether it is a thought, a person, or a belief.

I ask you to be specific in your life. Take the time to write down what is hindering you. However, do not stop there. Next, ask God to remove the hindrances. Ask God to give you his strength to remove yourself from the hindrances and never return to that place again. Know the mountain is no longer a mountain, it is now a testimony.

The reward for having that testimony is someday, you may encounter someone who is being challenged by the same mountain you once had. You'll be able to advise that person on the best way to speak to that mountain and have it removed with your verbal testimony.

There is value to speaking joy over your life and the life of family, friends, and loves ones. I cannot say this enough.

Verbal Soil

₪ (POTT) I, (insert name here), am stronger, wiser, and better as of right now.

"It is your heart, not the dictionary that gives meaning to your words. A good person produces good deeds and words season after season. An evil person is blight on the orchard. Let me tell you something: Every one of these careless words is going to come back to haunt you. There will be a time of Reckoning. Words are powerful; take them seriously Words can be your salvation. Words can also be your damnation." (Matthew 12:34-37, The Message//Remix, New Testament IN Contemporary Language).

Be aware: there are words, there is soil, and when using the tongue, let's refer to the soil as verbal soil. A person's heart determines his speech. Your words reflect your fate—either you will be justified by them or condemned; damned by them.

Instead of pointless conversations, accept every opportunity that you talk with another person as an opportunity to speak on and accept what God has given you in your life, and SPEAK forward on what is to come. Use your words (verbal soil) as a possibility to reach others and sow into their lives for the better.

Verbal soil, when nurtured with good seed—which includes scripture, positive feedback, encouraging words, uplifting recommendation, and suggestions—will bring about high yield. Try not to get discouraged when you are changing your way of speaking. It might take time for others to get used to it, but faithfully speak life as often as possible.

Some people will respond differently because there are times in our lives when we are at different states of readiness. There is a possibility that many, if not a few, will be hardened by your living, loving words, and faithful scriptures. Some will not care, and others will be receptive.

Allow your WORDS to take root in your life. Just make sure your verbal soil is productive and fertile. Do not allow verbal weeds (negative talk, doubt) to take root. What comes out of the mouth gets its very start in the heart. Instead, push forward and upward with foundational words—words to build a life on.

Use the words in the Bible to build a life on, work them into your life, and sooner than you know, you will be living everything that you are saying! Now, that is exciting!!

Word of Mouth

Talk Away!!!

Talk away encourages you to keep talking until you cannot talk anymore, especially when you are talking in positive and motivating ways.

As a parent of two lovable, blessed, and cherished children, I feel it is right for me to hit on the subject, "Word of Mouth." I feel my children are very special, and so is everyone else's.

Word of Mouth is important to me, especially when I am in the presence of my children and other young children I mentor and teach. I speak value into the lives of younger children as at a young age, this is when developing a sense of who they are and what they want to become begins to play an important role. Words of consideration can prevent our youth from developing low self-esteem and a mind-set of disappointments.

As an active, compassionate parent, my goal is to instill solid core values and assist in creating an advanced self-positive image, along with engaging in honest and sincere conversations with my younger peers.

Presently, there is not an instruction manual for creating the perfect self-assured child. However, as a motivated parent, I would advise speaking life over the youth and engage in several ways to nurture and grow a strong sense of "YOU CAN," "YOU WILL," "YOU ARE SMART," etc.

We as parents, mentors, and adults should want our youth to have a strong sense of self-value as they grow and develop. The challenge that often comes with youth is they are listening more than they are talking. Thus, our job is to reassure we are speaking as motivators and inspiring them from birth. Parts of the early lessons must include all the ways to love and embrace our youth verbally.

It's never too early to start. Get in the habit of complementing your children. The words that come from parents are very important and are hidden treasures. Your words are blessings upon their lives. As children, we all have looked for approval from adults. How much farther could one child go when he/she hears they are **important**, they are **special,** they are **beautiful,** and they are **loved**?

Do not allow the tongue to have a lack of verbal inspiration when it comes to children. You want your boy or girl to be smarter, faster, more intellectual, dynamic, and self-motivated than you ever were. Let it start with inspiring guidance.

In this life, there are no repeat buttons. Advise your children and youth by teaching them to speak value into their lives and into the lives of others. Developing positive talk and inspirational guidance early on has the potential to encourage the significance of others.

Aim for developing high self-esteem and trust with words that are essential to build the child to the best that they are capable of being. Allow the WORD FROM THE MOUTH to be the very great and lifted WORDS OF MOUTH to inspire, to love, and to lead.

In Proverbs 22:6, it says, "*Train a child in the way he should go: and when he is old, he will not depart from it.*"

As we are training, let's inspire with words of encouragement and structure. Children are our future; let's speak greatness and chance over our future leaders.

Talk is Cheap

Talk can be very cheap at times, especially talk that is nonproductive, unconstructive, harmful, and negative. It can also be like promising much with the tongue and producing nothing.

Talk can become very valuable when you decide to speak happiness and reward in favor of better—speak in favor for the good of all. Commit to memory the scripture according to Romans 8:28, *"All things work together for those that Love the Lord."*

If you love me (the Lord), show it by doing what I told you to do. This is given to us according to John 14:15. Do yourself a favor and commit to what he spoke concerning your tongue and how you use your tongue.

I know you might want to confess that this sounds like a verbal fairy tale. I would agree if I did not know any better, yet his word is truer than anything that ever existed. *"Let the words of my mouth and the meditation of my heart; be acceptable in thy sight, O Lord, my strength, and my redeemer."* (Psalms 19:14).

Use your verbal skills to encourage; the creator does not encourage a negative tongue. He even protects us from the act of others speaking of non-trust and against another according to Psalms 31:20, *"thou shalt keep them secretly in a pavilion from the strife of tongues."*

By shifting the mind and then adjusting the attitude, you can use the tongue to fight against negative thoughts, negative people, and negative situations using the tongue as the sword of the mouth.

Maintain a growing relationship with your tongue. Spend time daily reading and speaking quotes and scriptures, reciting literature that that is uplifting, *"For the word of the Lord is right; and all his works are done in truth."* (Psalm 33:4).

Spend time with others who articulate with the power of God's words and time with those who carry a better verbal outlook on life. This is a way to develop and appreciate constant verbal improvement. Talk is cheap when one speaks fear, defeat, doubt, and destruction.

My late inspiring father, Sammy Ivery, would always tell me, "Go have Fun." No matter what the situation or the circumstance was, he would always remind me to have fun. As I was competing in track for John Tyler High School in Tyler, Texas, and continued to compete at Baylor University in Waco, Texas, before every performance, my dad would call me, or when he was present, he would pat and hug me while reminding me to have fun. At that time in my life I wanted to scream and ask him, "Are you out of you mind? This sport with intense training seems to hurt me not only physically, but mentally from thinking and focusing, and you want me to have fun?" Well, yes he did, even as he was leaving Earth, he kept reminding me to have fun.

Therefore, I have come to the conclusion that the more you have fun doing anything in this world, the enjoyment you create while doing it helps you to become better at doing what you are attempting to master. The more joy you speak about being alive and alert and blessed in more ways than one, the better you will succeed and accomplish greater things in life, in your career, with your family, and with your social connections.

The more you speak life and speak about elevating and inspirational life experiences and circumstances instead of doubts and hassles, you shall notice more power, energy, and enthusiasm for living and striving to be better than you were yesterday.

Instead of just speaking it, you will be living it the majority of your life. One of the best approaches to life is to speak it into existence. Should you choose to speak victory, be also ready to receive victory!

Tell Me

₪ (POTT): I, (insert name here), am somebody because I am a child of God.

Tell me, what makes you, you? What makes you so special there is nothing or anyone who can cause you to doubt in your mind that you're nothing less than great, beautiful, chosen, and loved?

It is so very simple to believe better and receive better. It is NOT necessary to make it complicated or difficult to accept you are a child of God, you have purpose, and with the time that is given, it is better to speak and perform, speak and achieve, speak and succeed.

There is an option available to you and the option is to "Tell Me." Tell Me is a verbal approach I suggest you use. This is when you take a look at yourself every day, speak to yourself, and tell yourself the truth. Tell yourself that, *"God created man in his own image, in the image of God created him; male and female, you are the creation that was and is separate and distinct from all previous creations."*

You are an amazing **creative** work of God. Given the power that is deep down within, you are capable of becoming a creative genius. As you speak greater, you will start to understand the God-like, God-resembling attributes that are endowed in you.

If you have a best friend, a girlfriend, a boyfriend, a wife, husband, a son or daughter, a niece or a nephew, have daily ambition to look at that person or speak to that person over the phone or by email, whatever the form of communication may be. Encourage that person and let them hear you tell them they are no less than a child of God, the most-high God.

Use your tongue to make a difference around you. Start at home, start at work, start on social media; the point is to start now—every time you come across and in touch with the numerous people in your life.

Day after day, there are people who will tell you how they feel, and the feeling is usually opposite of being loved and adored, successful and accomplished. For some, it is a constant struggle and a hassle to think positive never mind speak positive, so where do you come in? Your verbal approach is capable of helping another become powerful and uplifted.

Remember, "TELL ME" is reminding oneself or that other person how great they are and how great they are capable of becoming. The "Tell Me" approach transitions to an attitude of excitement.

The Power of your tongue is stunning and beautiful. You can be excited about life when the way you speak reflects positive, stronger formation. On the other hand, misery talk loves company, so pick up your bags and **do not allow** that place as your personal residence. Instead, talk and promote life with the power of words.

Speak with positive expectancy and optimistic possibility to lift your energy levels. In doing so, there is practically no boundary to what you can and will accomplish. This is magnificent!

The power in the tongue is a matter of character and attitude. You can turn the most mundane of past experiences in life around by speaking forward with intention. Speak with emotion, speak with courage, speak open-minded, speak past fear, and speak past and beyond what is uncomfortable for you.

There are a million miracles happening all around the world. Many may not agree because they do not want to accept that they are not looking for the miracles or speaking the miracles into their lives. So here is the "Tell Me" approach for you—you are great! Continue to grow and smile! It is getting better as you read on.

Verbal Residence

₪ (POTT): I, (insert name here), will speak as if positive things are happening to me. Invigorating and uplifting opportunities are coming my way.

Verbal Residence are words that belong in the heart. Give these words home in your heart; speak them into your life and into the lives of others.

Amazing, Awesome, Abundant, Abundance, Accomplished, Achievable, Active, A Reason for Being, Blessed, Beautiful, Bold, Believe, Caring, Capable, Cheerful, Confident, Courteous, Connected, Cheerful, Desire, Enjoy, Elevated, Energy, Fantastic, Fun, Friendly, Forgiveness, Faith, Generous, Glory, Guidance, God, Good, Hope, Healthy, Heavenly, Humble, Honesty, Holy, Infinite, Intelligent, Inspired, Joy, Life, Love, Motivational, Motivated, Mercy, Miracle, Magnificent, Meditation, Modest, Nurturing, New, Nice, Outstanding, Optimistic, Obedient, OK, Opportunity, Oneness, Positive, Power, Perseverance, Pure, Patience, Preserved Progress, Peace of Mind, Positive, Powerful, Purpose, Power, Quality, Radiant, Rejuvenated, Renewed, Reborn, Reliable, Relieved, Righteousness, Sustained, Still, Strength, Super, True, Trust, Thankful, Transformed, Team work, Triumph, Unique, Uplift, Upgrade, Understanding, Vitality, Vibes, Value, Victorious, Vibrant, Victory, Virtuous,

Worth, Worthy, Welcome, Wise, Wonderful, Well, Wisdom, Yes, Youthful, Young, Zealous, Zesty.

This is just my personal list of words that I include in my personal conversations about others and with others. I realize words have meaning, and when I speak, I intend to speak with purpose. I intend to inspire and encourage by including in my vocabulary inspirational words that create positive feelings which creates positive thinking, which promotes growth.

Words can be the key to making your life an adventure. Create a list of words on the next page that you would like to include in your conversations concerning your dreams, hopes, and desires. Trust your words and trust your decisions. Do not allow the wrong words to hold you back.

miracles	
Divine Substance	
Divine arrangement	
Christ	
Holy Spirit	
Victory	
Victorious	
Successful	
Full of Joy	
Love	
Romance	
World Records	
National Records	

Simply Speaking

What are you looking forward to saying?

Keep yourself and others motivated. Do not allow your words to paralyze your dreams, desires, and life goals. Get rid of negative and unhealthy speaking. Instead, learn and lean on the power of scripture and the power of your words.

Say goodbye to "I can't," "It never will," and "It is impossible." Instead, fill your speaking with life and creativity. Every day is a new day to create a Verbal Resolution. Cut out the negative word play and include the positive as much as possible.

Learn to say goodbye to trying to do it others' way. You know what is in your heart. Most of the time, it is the words that come out of your mouth. No one else can live your life and speak better over your life better than you are able to do.

Look forward to leaving behind the little voice in your head that reminds you, "You do not know enough," "You don't deserve better," and "You can't do it." Simply ignore them and speak the truth. You are learning as you live. You do deserve better, and you can do it.

Feel positive and celebrate yourself verbally, celebrate who you are now, and who you are transitioning to be.

Keep telling yourself you are going to celebrate being you! Verbally thank yourself for willing to grow, for willing to push forward, for willing to enlighten yourself as well as others.

The tongue is for more than just tasting—the tongue has a purpose to feed your soul. Verbally count the ways that you are blessed. It can be a new workout for you. Now, repeat after me: "Here's to positive speaking, to speaking faith, and to speaking life.

Keep in mind, "One word can make all the difference."

Spreading the Word

This is your moment! I am pretty sure there are many people who want to hear great news from you, great inspiration from you, and positive feedback from you. I am sure you can relate to a conversation you have had with a friend, a neighbor, coworker, family members, and others.

You may recall conversing with someone, and while talking, instead of lifting that person up, you took the turn to make matters worse or at a standstill by being negative. I am guilty of having conversations like that in the past, which is why it is so important that we make time for verbal reflection.

We must remember we are constantly growing and evolving. Nothing is permanent, and as we continue to correct and push forward no matter what, verbal obstacles may confront us. As we grow and learn to encourage, even in our earnest moments of hesitation of doubt, we will start to talk ourselves and others forward, where destiny—our destiny—abundantly intends for us to be.

Resolve to speaking life in easier ways; it will make life easier. The future will not wait, so re-talk it while you can. Start to focus, look in your mirror, accept where you are, who you are, and reconnect. The very person you are looking at is the person who will get you to understand and appreciate life. Speak to your life and expect better outcomes. Speak it moment by moment. You are what you speak, so speak life.

The power of your tongue is the creator of your world.

Speak perfection.

The Power of the Tongue.

Tongue Testimony

God, help me to see you at work in ways I would have missed. I have been blessed in so many ways.

If your mind is heavy and you are looking for a better way to become more effective with your creator, then create a better way to speak, create a better way to acknowledge your situations, speak life into your dreams, and speak life into your situations.

Do not talk lowly of yourself or others. Do not doubt God; do not worry (Matthew 6:34). The Power of the Tongue is just about getting your sentences to come out right.

It is a focus on healthy and conscious verbal flow; no more babbling; no more unhealthy words or sentences. Instead, it is time to speak truth, want, direction, positively to every situation.

Where are you headed? It is not a deceptive question. Confidently respond, "I am headed up!" When you talk, your mind and concerns are listening, so speak well.

The Power of the Tongue will meet you right where you are and lead you to discover the very power of the tongue. The Lord has already given us the blueprint—all we have to do is repeat after him and believe that we are built to believe, to achieve, to conquer, and to excel.

Allow the journey to begin with the right words. Keep speaking sentences that are conducted with purpose, encouraging intention, acknowledging greatness, and fostering determination to **be better** than yesterday**, to speak** better, and to **push forward** toward a greater tomorrow.

In conclusion…

…our God is totally amazing… *"Old things are passed away, behold, all things are become new."* (2 Corinthians 5:17)

Speak life into your situations.

In this book, I attempted to express to you that faith is real; faith can be spoken moment by moment, believed moment by moment, received moment by moment. Just know it takes patience and persistence to accomplish faith. It is stated in Romans 12:2, *"Be Ye transformed by the renewing of your mind."* May I add that the renewing of your mind will transform the tongue that translates to you speaking better words that create better chances.

La Kadron Ivery

To contact the author,
email: thepowerofthetongue33@gmail.com